sKeptSinging

urpleOurBruis

sKeptSinging

urpleOurB

uisesK Sing

gPu Our

ruisesKeptSing

gPu

Malcolm Friend

ruises ing

gPurpleOur

ruisesKeptSin

Our Bruises Kept Singing Purple
Copyright 2018 by Malcolm Friend
ISBN: 978-1-7324032-0-8
Library of Congress Control Number: 2018950334


Cover art: "Carivalesco" by Wichie Torres
Book design and layout by Lawrence Eby

Printed and bound in the United States
Distributed by Ingram

Published by Inlandia Institute
Riverside, California
www.inlandiainstitute.org
First Edition

# Our Bruises Kept Singing Purple

Malcolm Friend

## Contents

The Bomba Man and The Blues Man walk into a bar 1

WHAT PHANTOMS DANCE IN MY EYES 3

Afro-Seattleite Fragment #12: South End Conditioning 5
Afro-Seattleite Fragment #3: Silver Fork (An Elegy) 7
Why I Can't Watch Any Videos Where Black People Are Attacked 9
Afro-Seattleite Fragment #11: My Brother's Laughter 10
El Moro 13
On Being Told I Look Like the Rapper J. Cole, or List of Black People I Apparently Look Like, or Do All Black People Look Alike? 15
Because Mom Doesn't Sing Every Song by The Temptations 17
Lamento Borincano 19
Promesa 21
Lamento en bolero (Clemente's Pain) 22
Because the Animal Has Always Been Human To Me (Or Maybe the Human Has Always Been Animal) 25
Afro-Seattleite Fragment #20: Ode To Russell Wilson, or Because These Respectability Politics Ain't Never Saved Us 27
Afro-Seattleite Fragment #17: Love Letter To Macklemore 28
Ode To Zion & Lennox in Which I Consider My Dad otra vez, Ending on a Lyric by Cheo Feliciano 30
Failed Blues 32
Afro-Seattleite Fragment #9: Ode To Rainier Beach 34

WHERE EVERY SUENA RESTS 37

Reggaetón as Sensible Form of Puerto Rican Therapy, or A Close Listening of Don Omar's "Hasta abajo" 39
Afro-Seattleite Fragment #6: Prayer in the Mode of Sir 42

Mix-a-Lot's "Posse on Broadway," or South End Kid Returns To Capitol Hill Six Years after Graduating High School
Clemente al Sonero Mayor: Elegy in Bomba 44
malcolm meets tite curet alonso at hemingway's café, pittsburgh, 47
Afro-Seattleite Fragment #4: Ezell's Chicken 48
Failed Bomba 50
Afro-Seattleite Fragment #1: Black Kid, White City 52
Orpheus as El incomprendido 54
Encyclopedia Entry: Afro-Seattleite, 55
Four-Dollar Mofongo, or On Having to Explain Why Puerto Rico Uses American Dollars 56
Rice and Beans 59
Ode To Bob Marley, Ending in Inheritance 62
Afro-Seattleite Fragment #21: Jamal Crawford, or Ode To the Crossover 63
Afro-Seattleite Fragment #8: Ken Griffey, Jr., or The Sweetest Swing 64
El Conde Sings "Babaila" 66
Afro-Seattleite Fragment #15: Jimi Hendrix Plays "The Star-Spangled Banner" – Woodstock, 1969 67

CASTAWAY MUSIC 69

Bomba-Blues Dream Sequence 71
Bomba-Blues Noise Report 73
The Bomba Man Talks Shit To Malcolm 74
America 76
The Blues Man Talks Shit To Malcolm 79
Ode To Stevie Wonder, or Mom Calls Me after Milwaukee and All I Can Do Is Listen To "I Wish" 81
Ode To the Barbershop 84
Poem in Which Marcus Stroman Addresses Puerto Rico on the Issue of His Puertorriqueñidad, Revolving Around a Line from Tato Laviera 85
The Bomba Man and The Blues Man Argue Over Who Has 86

to Bury Malcolm's Body
Grifería: Clemente Responds To Luis Palés Matos 87
Afro-Seattleite Fragment #19: Ode To Gabriel Teodros, or Mixed Kid Learns to Sing 89
Fried 90
Prayer as Don Omar 95
Ode To La Sista, or I Listen To *Majestad negroide* and Reread Palés Matos 96
Ode To Tego Calderón, or The Day *El abayarde* Dropped Was Maelo's Resurrection 98
Afro-Seattleite Fragment #18: When I Found Out *Cold Hearted in Cloud City* Is a Love Letter To the South End 99

Notes 101
Acknowledgments 103
About the Author 107
About the Inlandia Institute 109

*for Mom and Dad*
*for Nini, Veronica, and Marques*
*for Gabby*

urBruisesKept
ruisesKept Sing
sKept Singing Pu
nging Purple Ou
g PurpleOur Bru
leOur OurBruises
OurBruisesKept
ruisesKept Sing
sKept SingingPu
ngingPurpleOurB
urple OurBruises
urBruisesKept Sin

*for our blood, mixed*
*soon with their passion in sport,*

*in indifference, in anger,*
*will create new soils, new souls, new*
*ancestors*

—Kamau Brathwaite

# The Bomba Man and The Blues Man walk into a bar,

the one with a barrel drum
strapped heavy on his back,
the other dragging guitar in hand,
and I'm thinking
this has got to be a joke, right?
Like some next level
negro bembón
chewing on some strange fruit type shit,
some niche meets negro spiritual shit.

Then The Bomba Man orders rum
and The Blues Man orders cognac
and I'm cracking up
'cause I know how this ends.
This ends with *si Dios fuera negro*
and *dark gon' catch me here.*
This ends with *he sufrido, compaí*
and *I'se felt pain.*
I know this ends
exactly how it started:
with black tears
and black scars

and the whole thing is hilarious
until the two sit down
on either side of me.

I look to both
and can see into their liquor,
catch sight of bones floating
where ice should be
and realize I can't move.

The Bomba Man shifts his drum.
The Blues Man lifts his guitar.

*Chamaquito, mandan que cantes.*

*They want your song, boy.*

And now I know this is a joke
and the punchline is me.

*He played that sad raggy tune like a musical fool.*
*Sweet Blues!*

—Langston Hughes

# Afro-Seattleite Fragment #12: South End Conditioning

*I'm right back where I started / in the South of the city where the rain and my heart is.*

—Khingz, "Prodigal"

The South of the city—that's where your heart is.
You always end up right back where you started.

When Daniel runs after you, the echo marches,
and you don't even realize how frantic your heart is.

You're no longer on Pitt's campus. Head arches
and you're in the South of the city, where your heart is.

Sweat cakes your M's t-shirt. You become guarded,
tense your whole body tight like a muscle—like your heart is.

Thought these poems would save you, but your art is
product of the South of the city—always where your heart is.

Stomp of footsteps louder, your hands dip into pockets,
slip keys between fingers. How still your heart is.

How easy it is. Making yourself weapon. Becoming heartless.
Is that the South of the city? Is that where your heart is?

When Daniel runs after you, think of how he'd have darted
if you'd hit him, stained your shorts red like your heart is.

Remember winter mornings. 6 AM bus rides. Streetlight hum
charting
your presence in the South of the city. The machine your heart is.

Shake Daniel's hand. Let him compliment your poems. Play bard and
act like the keys in your pocket ain't where your heart is.

Laugh. Like you did most South End mornings. You know the hardest part is
forgetting the South of the city. Can't do that. That's where your heart is.

# Afro-Seattleite Fragment #3: Silver Fork (An Elegy)

1.

It's 1995, maybe '96.
Truth is you'll be here so often
before you reach twenty-one
that Silver Fork will be associated
with the beginning of time.

When you're six, you'll come here
after your younger sister busts the top
of your first adult tooth, an incisor.

At nineteen you'll bring your best friend
from high school here,
sink your teeth into a Soul Burger.

But for now you're three, maybe four.
Diana Ross is asking where her love went
and Dad's ordered you a short stack,
more food than you'll actually eat.

You order the hot chocolate yourself.
A Mt. Rainier portion of whipped cream
looms over the cup's horizon,
and you'll spend more time forcing spoonful
after spoonful of it into your mouth
than eating what little portion of your pancakes
you don't fork over to Dad.

2.

It's 2010.
You've just graduated from high school.
Four generations of your blood
have gathered here:

Marte, Mom and Dad,
Marques, Veronica, Nini (with Will),
and Junior.

Your nephew is two,
just a couple years younger than you were
the first time you stepped in here.
This time it's David Ruffin
insisting he ain't too proud to beg
but the story is the same:

he smiles, he laughs,
he eats some (but not all)
of his pancakes, and for a moment
you think this is a family inheritance.

In barely three years
Silver Fork will close,
the land used instead
for a Safeway gas station.
Your nephew is the last of your lineage
to ever be serenaded by Motown legends
as he eats breakfast,

and you wonder:
if he knew
would he commit the moment to memory
or would he sit there,
smile sitting on top of his face,
just like you did years ago
when they brought that hot chocolate,
whipped cream bursting
over the edge of the cup?

## Why I Can't Watch Any Videos Where Black People Are Attacked

I don't like to play make-believe with this very real body. I can't even watch *Glory* all the way through. Skip the scene where Denzel is whipped—can't remember it's not actually Denzel, not his scars on his back, the beauty of make-up. Single tear slow rolling down his cheek the beauty of make-believe. I don't like to play make-believe with this very real body, something about seeing pain inflicted on someone who looks like me, who I'm trained to imagine looks like me. Imagine for a second your lover watches someone who looks like you murdered, begs to move somewhere they won't kill us and you can't imagine that place exists. Every night you sleep with corpses in your bed, see your face in every one of them, wonder how your bed became coffin, mass grave. I keep hearing these videos are important, necessary—see friends posting them. Saying we need them. How else will people know what's happening? I want to say I already know. I always have. Why can't you tell?

# Afro-Seattleite Fragment #11: My Brother's Laughter

*for Marques Friend*

1. As Kids

...is pure joy
when I first hear it—
the feeling of Dad's bedtime stories
or when Mom sings along to Stevie.

Is hearing my first prayer
(or maybe just the first I remember)
answered so that I am no longer
simply stuck between two sisters.

Is reminder not to complain
when Mom makes you take him
to the park and he's thrilled
with how high you can push him
on the swings.

Is in tune
with the red rubber turtle
I bounce along
the side of his crib,
or the swing of my head
he'll still find funny
as a teenager.

Is success.
Is learning at the age of four
that I am a good older brother.

2. The First Time I'm Stopped by the Cops

...is fear.

Not his, but my own.
The tears I stifle
and the echo in my head:
*Don't break Mom's heart.*
*Don't become a statistic.*

Is jagged knife
of the officer's hand
against my cold-stiffened legs
and torso, searching for a gun
I'd never dare to have
while his partner rifles
through my backpack.

Is my jagged breath
when the officer feels
the CD player (gun)
in my pocket
and demands to know (gun)
what it is (gun).

Is my empty pride
when his partner asks
if I've ever been in trouble
with the cops before
and I say No.

Is confusion when he responds
*You don't have to worry about that*
*for another five years,*
as if this is rite of passage
never grown out of.

(Is remembering his words
when it happens again

five years later
in a Spanish train station,
knowing I am most colored
against navy-clad backgrounds.)

Is Dad's growled order
for my brother not to laugh
when my venting
becomes cautionary tale,
his scolding that this is serious.

Is knowing
when I wish it'll happen to him
just so he'll understand,
I am the worst older brother.

# El Moro

Your skin absorbs
thick Alicante air
in the midst of festival.
You have finally
figured your way back home
and are approaching the door
when you see finger flung
in your direction.

Skin tingles
as if that finger is a blade
slicing down your chest
but you keep your eyes
focused ahead,
pick up your pace.
You know what is coming.
Soco has warned you
that the hoguera flames
ignite a special kind of fire
in Alicante streets.
But even before that,
you knew.
This skin has always known.
Still, his words
slice open the wound.

*Yo quiero una foto*
*con el moro.*

In an instance
you are no longer you,
no longer person.
His finger jabs through you,
Lets you know this skin
says you are thing.

You are desired
object. You are prop
in Reconquista reenactment,
his little Moor.
This skin is inscribed,
tells him history.

Your stomach begins to churn.
You fumble your keys
as you struggle with the lock,
with a stranger's words,
an accusing finger shot into you.
You won't tell him
the histories he inscribes
are not yours.
Instead, you blame pints
poured down your throat
earlier that evening in ecstasy.

Problem is
the sour of bile:
the next morning
as music from the street
floods your room;
the next week
as you return home;
the next month
when you move to Pittsburgh.

This nausea stays bubbling
in your gut,
through your throat,
on your flesh.

# On Being Told I Look Like the Rapper J. Cole, or List of Black People I Apparently Look Like, or Do All Black People Look Alike?

I suppose it doesn't bite as much as any of the other names white
folks have thrown at me:

K'naan, Steph Curry, Colin Kaepaernick, Drake—Black boys I
know I look nothing like.

I suppose it's better than all my high school classmates who said

I looked like Nathan Peoples, one of the only other Black kids in
our year,

or the time Matt, the PhD student I did a project with, mistook
Cameron Barnett for me—

I suppose it's better than the woman who told Cameron he looks
like Philly's Mayor Nutter

although I suppose by the transitive property of mistaken identity
I look like Mayor Nutter?

But let me not make this completely about white folks and the
haunts they conjure,

used to Black folks becoming Black ghosts. Real talk, only Black
folks say I look like Cole:

niggas shouting *Cole World* from across Alumni Lawn in college,

high school poets we mentored taking joke photos, insisting I do
his sideways peace sign.

And I'm reminded of the time I was riding the 7 through Columbia
City

and an immigrant asked *Ethiopia? Ethiopia? Ethiopia?* until I finally realized

he was talking to me and believe when I said no his response was *Eritrea?*

In Pittsburgh I'm asked if my name is Charles, if I'm Steve's brother, all by Black folks,

and because I have no known family here, no bed of bones to fall back on,

I'm forced to wonder what phantoms dance in my eyes or maybe theirs—

these hauntings from histories that ain't ours but are with every new dead Black boy:

Trayvon Martin, Mike Brown, Freddie Gray, Tamir Rice, and... and...and...and...

and one time Cole did a song for one of those Black boys, which is to say he did a song

for all of those Black boys, which is to say I know he did the song for himself because

I see Cole's face in photos of Black people protesting. See my own face in Cole,

mutual haunting I've learned to expect. Which is to say I wonder if our faces will ever stop

bleeding together, if we'll ever stop bleeding together, if we'll ever stop bleeding.

# Because Mom Doesn't Sing Every Song by The Temptations

*Must be something bad in his blood.*
*Did you feel it—*
*his hands tugging at my scalp*
*when Derek put you on the phone?*
*Did your neck rubberband-*
*snap like mine when he called you*
*Rion's boy?*

*I told you how I cut my hair*
*the day after he grabbed it.*
*How I imagined the flat-ironed strands*
*that fell to the floor as dirt*
*covering his coffin.*

*Did you dead-eye*
*your Uncle Derek like I did*
*your grandfather*
*after he noticed that haircut?*

*I hope you did.*
*He had no right*
*putting you on the phone*
*with that man.*
*You ain't his kid, after all.*
*The nerve of him.*
*And on Thanksgiving, no less.*

*Like Derek doesn't remember*
*the Thanksgiving he locked us out*
*in the Chicago cold, wind*
*a snake coiling around us,*
*venom that broke the blood*
*of his marriage.*

*Do you understand now*

*how your grandfather*
*has always been a rollin' stone?*
*Something bad in his blood.*
*Same thing makes you tap your foot*
*to "Papa Was a Rollin' Stone"*
*no matter how still*
*I sit, like you can't tell I still*
*taste his venom*
*crowding my spit*
*when the grit and gravel*
*of Dennis Edward's voice*
*falls into those horns.*

*Don't know I tried to suck*
*that venom out you and your siblings.*
*Bit into each of you*
*the day you were born,*
*hoped the poison*
*would flow out your veins.*

*Tell me, Mal,*
*Did it work?*

## Lamento Borincano

*—after Rafael Hernández*

*yo soy tu hijo, / de una migración, / pecado forzado*

—Tato Laviera, "nuyorican"

*Sale loco de contento con su cargamento*
*para la ciudad*
*para la ciudad*

Dad is two or three, carried by abuela
through hallways with the stench of bacalao.

He smiles at the smell, or maybe he cries—
I don't really know, can't know. What I do:

Dad will mythologize this city, tell stories
like how he made fun of other people's Spanish,

the white woman who mistook *excitada* for *emocionada.*
This is how Dad is Puerto Rican.

*Todo todo está desierto y el pueblo está lleno*
*de necesidad*
*de necesidad*

Every couple winters Dad visited abuela's family,
picked mangos from the tree in his abuela's yard.

He swears the fruit was sweeter, that he complained
the entire plane ride back to New York.

But he never went back. Never thought to take his family.
Hopes his bedtime stories were enough to replace coquís

singing lullabies—reasons he never had either,
had to find another definition of boricua.

*Y triste    el jibarito va    pensando así*
*diciendo así    llorando así*
*por el camino*

Sometimes I wonder what would've happened
if abuela hadn't died here, if the cancer hadn't

rotted her inside-out, killed her like
one of her mother's overripe mangos.

I wonder if that's how Dad learned this climate
wasn't made to cultivate us, that the mangos

would always be sweeter allá, over those waters.
I wonder if that's when he decided he wouldn't

go back.

*Borinquen    ahora que tú te mueres*
*con tus pesares*
*déjame que te cante yo también*

## Promesa

*—after Romeo Santos, Usher, and the US govt.*

*To the inhabitants of Porto Rico:*
*In the prosecution of the war against the Kingdom of Spain by the people of the United States in the cause of liberty, justice, and humanity, its military forces have come to occupy the island of Porto Rico. They come bearing the banner of freedom, inspired by a noble purpose...to promote your prosperity.*

—Nelson A. Miles, 1898

*Tú cuerpo es la cárcel.*
Do I have to tell you of the prisoners,

of Albizu Campos, or López Rivera,
or abuela, trapped forever in a tomb

in Miami, came to this country
promised an American Dream,

cancer the nightmare she never woke up from?
*Tienes control sobre mí*, mi isla, the bombs

dropped over Vieques—I hear skeletons rattling
when Caribbean waves reach shore.

Has this always been your promise?
For my joints to be crushed into sand?

For the waves to be my only elegy?
*I'll give you my heart, but you gotta promise:*

*promise you'll hold me* when these nerves
finally settle into themselves again.

*Prométeme que no me vas a dejar*
without at least promise of proper burial,
somewhere these bones can be left alone.

# Lamento en bolero (Clemente's Pain)

*for Cheo Feliciano and Michael Friend*

*For Clemente, those [salsa] moves were too fast, undignified, not cool enough, and he wasn't any good at them. He liked the Boleros, the slow dances.*
—David Maraniss, *Clemente: The Passion and Grace of Baseball's Last Hero*

*ay, que cansancio de todo*
*de seguir esperando*

Vic says
I can't dance salsa,
tells people
it's too fast:

"Ooh, baby.
Roberto dancing salsa?"

Tells people I got them piernas
made of piedra.
Says I'm too stoic,
too static to feel
enclosed lightning
sounding trumpets.

Says I'm too cool
for congas—
that's why I dance bolero.
He's wrong.

*ay, se acabó la esperanza*
*se perdió la confianza*

Forget about shifting hips
and frenetic feet.

Bolero
lets my limbs
hang languid,
brings my electric movement
to stasis. I languish
to a bolero-man's croon.

Bolero is the pinballing
disk in my back—
the pang as it pops
in and out of place;
it's the pinch in my neck
when I face pitchers,
the strain as my shoulder
drags heavy lumbered bat
across the plate;
it's the accusation
that I'm faking it all.

Bolero is every shot
at my accent
in the Pittsburgh papers:
"I hit many
what you call
'bad bol,'"
"We have good speerit
on Pirates thees' year,"
"I have friend
in Puerto Rica."

Bolero
is leaving Puerto Rico,
trading the blue
of the Caribbean
for the blues

of not having the words
to describe it.

Cántame,
cantante del bolero.
Que sigas trovando.
Bolero-man,
I'll dance your song,
feet dragging on pace
to your slow cadence,
if only because your throat
forces out mirror
reflecting my pain:

*ay, que cansancio en el alma*
*de esperar tu regreso*

*cansancio*

# Because the Animal Has Always Been Human To Me (Or Maybe the Human Has Always Been Animal)

Freshman year, my high school's Olympic Week has a "Hip Hop Day"

The mostly white student body jokes about dressing like hoodrats

asks the first Black student they can find for an extra basketball jersey

or durag and

in Season 1 of *Friday Night Lights*,

Smash Williams is called a junkyard dog

by one of his coaches

Only an animal could be as ferocious

as he is on the field and

it's ~~1960~~ ~~1970~~ ~~1980~~ ~~1987~~ ~~1988~~ ~~2006~~ ~~2009~~ ~~2010~~ ~~2011~~ ~~2013~~ ~~2014~~ 20--

and a banana is thrown at a black soccer player

in ~~England~~ ~~Scotland~~ ~~Spain~~ ~~France~~ ~~Turkey~~ ~~Mexico~~ ~~Russia~~ ~~Italy~~ ~~Germany~~

[Insert Name of Country Here] and

in 2014 I'm in Spain and a friend's bag is stolen while we aren't looking

When we ask someone nearby if he saw anything

he says the guy was a moro: *como tú* he points,

his finger a leash choking the Spanish
from my throat and

in 2016 a student of mine writes a racist paper

details how Black people have to resist their primal urge

to use vernacular in order to advance as a people and

every morning I greet the animal in the mirror

Its eyes lock on me, fixated, hunting, clawing out of the glass

It growls at me, calls me every name I've never been called

Says *you monkey, you dog, you hoodrat, you sloth*

Says *you nigger don't you know I've always been here*

*on the surface, your precious little mouthpiece?*

# Afro-Seattleite Fragment #20: Ode To Russell Wilson, or Because These Respectability Politics Ain't Never Saved Us

*I understand and respect the cause because there's so much going on in America right now....For me, I love the flag, I love the national anthem.*

—Russell Wilson

*Shouldn't this state*
*Have a song?*

*And shall we call it*
*My face will murder me?*

—Cornelius Eady, "Alabama, c. 1963: A Ballad by John Coltrane"

Russell, I know what it's like. I, too, once savored the taste of my tongue. Mom always made sure I spoke nice and proper, taught me to sandpaper anything pushing out these lips so my teeth wouldn't get chipped on the way out. In high school, I got good grades, studied hard for every test, took Shakespeare, wrote bad poems. Didn't stop the priests from telling me to pull my pants above the slivered waistband of my boxers while Ryan's hung below his ass. Didn't stop Smitty from rubbing his hands all over my hair, or calling *Black Out* whenever he wanted me to post up during pickup basketball games. Russell, what if I told you that freshman year of college, I chopped all of my hair off so no one could ever touch it again? That as I sat in the barbershop chair and my curls flattened on the floor like a deflated basketball I remembered sitting still at home in the basement, Dad trying to dissuade me from going to that high school? That a part of me wished I had listened, even as Auntie Bug bragged about the top 20 university that high school sent me to just like Mom does? Would you take it all to mean that I don't blame you? Don't expect you to prioritize the cloth covering a dirt-caked casket to the cloth of the flag? We swallow our tongues because no one else is putting food on our tables. How else we supposed to eat? We all just trying to stay fed.

## Afro-Seattleite Fragment #17: Love Letter To Macklemore

*—after Marcus Wicker*

Your music saved a shy Black boy
from conversation.
When I think of you,
it's usually morning carpools.
The absence of conversation
between me and Kevin,
how I kept wishing for the hour-long
bus rides because I could lean
against the window, no expectation
to talk to anyone.
I didn't really want to listen to you.
You were 2Pac minus
Black Panther parents,
Snoop Dogg raised in Capitol Hill.
At some point you seduced me.
Something about a white boy
owning his privilege
and condemning our city racist
eased the hours I spent
in your Capitol Hill.
And Kevin was Filipino,
so that meant something, right?
I rocked to "White Privilege"
and "Claiming the City,"
called them 206 anthems in college.
I could un-feel Smitty and Mark's
rough hands in my hair.
All those white boys
who buried their fingers
in my scalp, those shovels
digging into me,
thinking they'd find something
I was hiding. Claiming me.
Reminding me no space was mine,

not even this body, always trying
to un-nap my roots,
these clumps of hair
forming fists on my head,
this body curling into fist
on the bus back to the South End.
I never imagined you
as guilty,
mistook your attempts at penance
for confessions of love
and threw myself at you.
And isn't that,
your guilt earning my love,
isn't that the beauty
of seduction?

# Ode To Zion & Lennox in Which I Consider My Dad otra vez, Ending on a Lyric by Cheo Feliciano

A *Remezcla* article pines for the old days of reggaetón.
Blames J. Balvin made the genre soft.
"Otra vez" plays in my headphones.
As the synth mimics the calm of an ocean breeze
and Zion near-whispers the opening notes, I laugh.
As if a dembow couldn't be more
than flesh crashing together.
As if Zion & Lennox hadn't crowned themselves
reyes de romantiqueo years ago.
As if Zion wasn't always beggar
dressing bluenote supplication in drumbeat.
As if the scratch of Lennox's voice
wasn't proof of cries continually caught
in the grooves of his throat.

As if I haven't always been choking
my own song in this boombox throat,
another nigga too proud to admit his pain.
And I know I inherit this from my dad.
How afraid I was to be llorón in front of him
because I'd never seen him cry.

How when my brother was twelve
I told him not to cry over the girl
who shut her ears to his love songs
because there would be others.
Didn't know I would lock the door
to my bedroom six years later,
the night my college girlfriend decided my crooning
was now off-tune for her ears.
How I silently wailed unsung notes into a lullaby.
How I never told Dad about it.
Waited until I was seeing someone else

to drop the news, like there wasn't any pain to it,
like I hadn't begged the bluenote back
down my throat with every Zion & Lennox song.

But of course this man who used to live by his fists
would also pause anytime The Four Tops
or Cheo let a bluenote drift into the air,
had to have always known there was pain worse
than getting your ass beat, that at least the purples fade.
Mom told me once Dad jumped over a bush
to catch up to her stride and I don't know
how to reconcile that with the same man
who escorted someone out back
for dancing with Mom except maybe it's proof
we all want someone to hold us close that last dance.
Want someone who will squeeze us so tight
the bluenote can't help but drift out on our breath,
can't help but make us cry for the world to turn back
just once, give us a chance to let it out just once.

And once my love asked me
to give her the saddest fuck of all time,
told me to play some music to set the mood.
And as a Zion & Lennox tune echoed
I cried into her shoulder, held her like I knew
she wasn't leaving, let the dembow break me.
And in my head, Cheo crooning the tune
Dad always used to play:

*Andar con la pena      de que nadie sepa*
    *cuál es mi dolor.*
*Sentir mi problema      y vivir la vida*
    *con cara de amor.*
*Y con pesadumbre      contestarle al mundo*
    *que nada ha pasado.*

## Failed Blues

Write about Black stuff.

Write about the hood,
and ballin' and drive-bys
and drug dealers—
make sure you remove
the apostrophe from ballin
when you write about ballin.

Drop some bars.
Pac or Biggie
or Kendrick or Cole.

Write the word nigga.
(Is your mixed breed ass
even allowed to use it?)

Write it as many times as seems natural
(you know natural means excess):

Nigga Nigga Nigga Nigga
Nigga Nigga

You Black so listen
to white folks say nigga—

tell you they didn't mean you.
Don't nobody ever mean you.
Jumped in oil, deep-fried yourself
past the point of recognition.
You just unknown body
floating downriver.
Other even to Other.
No promise to fetch your body,
drain your lungs,

bury you proper.
That would be
claiming you.

Write about that.
Then repeat.

It ain't blues
if you don't repeat.

# Afro-Seattleite Fragment #9: Ode To Rainier Beach

*My heart says do it for the South End streets and parks.*
—Khingz, "F.U.T.U.R.E."

For the blues
of this gray-sky city,
the sweat-stained t's
sticking to the chest that labored
to keep your heart inside
after almost getting jumped,
the trembling twigs that replaced
your skinny legs.

For the skinny legs
that didn't let it happen,
learning to hop fences,
plop back down,
and speed through the South End.

For the South End,
the ball courts laced
from Genesee to Othello,
the shouts of "Souf *End!*"
pouring from every street,
from every boy.

For the boys
on Rainier and Wabash,
whose shouts mutated
from Black vernacular
to black African
languages over the years.

For Rainier,
winding concrete river
from the CD

to the South End,
all the way down to Henderson,
where men barked catcalls
to every woman whose hips protruded,
swayed just the way they liked;
where South End war stories
were exchanged,
accusations of *punk ass*
and *bitch ass*
and *you ain't real*
tainting reputations
across the street
from Rainier Beach High.

For Rainier Beach High,
the school clinging onto life
like the ivy clinging
to its blue-lettered walls,
school you took
the 7 and the 106 to avoid,
a simple act
seen as treason by any
who happened to board with you,
steps pounding concrete
as they stared you down.

For the concrete,
street names Vampire and Leech,
for all the blood it consumed—
from the lip you split on Cloverdale
to the skin of a teenager split
by bullets on Fisher—
every blood-soaked corner of Rainier.

For the corner of Rainier and Wabash,

the drug dealers who crept down
to avoid the cops,
the sharp snap of footsteps
snapping you from sleep—
how you don't sleep sometimes
because you can still hear the echo.

On those nights
when the echoes are loudest,
when the hum of streetlights
is drowned out by footsteps
pounding the pavement,
do it for Rainier Beach.

# WHERE EVERY SUENA RESTS

*un negrito melodía he came along*
*improvising bomba drums on dancer's feet*

—Tato Laviera

# Reggaetón as Sensible Form of Puerto Rican Therapy, or A Close Listening of Don Omar's "Hasta abajo"

1. *así ha'ta abajo soy yo.*

tonight
gimme a dark room
and some loud tunes
banging
over neon lights—
¡suelta!
that's right;
bump that shit,
that's my jam
tonight.
tonight, just keep the hits
coming.

that's
how i
get down.
with every demented note,
another
drop
of sweat
from this
anguished
body.

2. *yo sólo quiero ver tu booty / por la di'co modelando*

another
drop
of sweat
clings
to her
anguished

body,
tight dress
pressed against me—
my fix:
this dembow ground
into the dance floor,
our backs breaking
on beat.
we break
ourselves
to forget how broken
we really are,
always seeking remedy
laced over
a repetitive beat,
our repetitive beating—
this pegao
this guaya,
¡cuidao,
puñeta!
these bodies,
this breaking
this
beat.

3. *por eso andan revuelta*

this space
be our riot.
all over the dance floor
our revolution.
let's degrade,
sweat a little more,
sully these bodies
until we
are true sucios,
dirty as the music we dance to.

4. *pa' bailarla encendi'a*

let's rock
until our bodies burn
or
let's dance perreo
until we grind ourselves
into dust
or
fuck wax.
fuck being one more
burning candle
lit in prayer.
effaced with jesus,
mary,
some other patron saint
or
maybe this time,
instead of ascending
into heaven,
what little is left of us
can find the beat
of a snare drum,
pounding dembow
that never rests.

# Afro-Seattleite Fragment #6: Prayer in the Mode of Sir Mix-a-Lot's "Posse on Broadway," or South End Kid Returns To Capitol Hill Six Years after Graduating High School

Dear Heavenly Father,

Let no sucka crews try to test me today.

These muscles are still tense
from crossing my arms
all those years ago
when I wanted to swing them.

Don't know when
they might rubberband-snap,
sting the latest offender.

Don't know when this tongue
might bust my teeth
cursing someone out—

shrapnel the stray bits
in the listener's skull
after years of saying nothing

to insults of *your hair*
*feels like steel wool* and
T-Hunt saying *I don't swim*

*in the chocolate river*
when he told me he wasn't
attracted to Black girls and

folks always placing The Beatles
above Stevie Wonder—
have they even listened
to *Songs in the Key of Life?*

Dear Heavenly Father,

In the six years since graduation
I've only ventured past Dick's
two or three times.

Ain't got no posse
to back me up
if shit goes sideways.

I still remember my first day.
How my skeleton tried to crawl
out my skin on the bus

when Broadway turned into 10th,
almost made its way past my lips
but yo-yoed back

as the bus screeched to a stop on Miller.
How I told myself it was first-day nerves.
How I still do even though they lingered

past the second day and the second year
and the last day of class,
these bones one step closer

to abandoning this skin every day.
How I prayed no one would test me,
ask *So where do you live?*

Dear Heavenly Father,

I still call the way my hands tremble and tense up
prayer.

## Clemente al Sonero Mayor: Elegy in Bomba

*—after Tato Laviera*

*Todo fue una cosa del pueblo, del negro...Clemente empezó a repartir palos y nosotros entramos ahí, tú sabes, con nuestra música.*

—Ismael Rivera

*Mataron al negro bembón.*
*Mataron al negro bembón.*

It begins:
your voice,
scrape of güiro
interrupting horns.
Usually music
of energy
and shifting feet,
today black
Spanish notes
form noose
in reverse.

*Hoy se llora noche y día*
*porque al negrito bembón*
*todo el mundo lo quería.*

What happened
to ecuajey,
pana mío?
What happened
to the banging
barril voice
that told us
we were beautiful,
that black
was beautiful?

*E'conde la bemba*
*que ahí viene el matón.*
*E'conde la bemba*
*que ahí viene el matón.*

My feet stumble
over these notes
I think misplayed,
make me misplay
fly balls.
Maelo,
they tell me a black boy
is dead in Mississippi,
reverse
to black
Spanish notes.

*Huye, huye,*
*que huye guantón.*
*Mira, que por allá*
*viene panchón.*

And they wonder
why I say
I don't want to be treated
like a Negro.
They kill blacks
in this country,
sin causa, sin razón,
call it sheet music
to an orchestra
we never asked
to be part of.

*Y saben la pregunta*
*que le hizo al matón.*

Because it's always
the same question:
why?
What did we do
wrong?
As if
there was any way
to change this.
As if the answer
isn't always
the same:

*"Yo lo maté por ser*
*tan bembón."*

Y hoy
lo lloro
noche y día.

# malcolm meets tite curet alonso at hemingway's café, pittsburgh,

and of course i don't recognize him at first. by which i mean he looks like any other brother sipping on something hard in this bar. the only reason i notice him is the tints of white and gray in his beard and eyebrows. until i look a little closer and see it's really bits of bone speckled over on his face. and i lean in a little closer, can hear him humming notes from maelo, el conde, la lupe, cheo—all tunes he wrote. and so i sit next to him, order two more of what he's ordered and when i take a sip all i taste is molasses but the more i drink the more i can hear him. two sips and the hum is louder. three and i can hear lyrics. four and a whole ocean starts to sway with each tune—every note becomes driftwood piecing itself back together into a boat. and i get to the bottom of the glass but instead of leftover ice there are iron-wrought chains. and i want to jerk my body away but i still feel this ocean swaying all through my nerves and he's looking back at me so i order two more drinks instead. and we keep drinking. and i'm all seasick but he sits steady. and i try to ask *don tite, why are you doing this?* but the words come out all slurred and dizzy. and the ceiling starts spinning. and his songs start pounding around my skull. and as i'm about to fall off my stool he grabs my arm. says *¿entiendes, m'ijo? this is what it means to channel the ancestors. this is how your body becomes theirs. can you handle it, all that sloshing in the pit of your stomach?*

# Afro-Seattleite Fragment #4: Ezell's Chicken

Yeast always rising—
it was never really about the chicken.

Coach Scott tells the BSA
we need something
to lure the white student body
to our events.

Someone seated in the back
yells Ezell's
and we dive in,
let the breath rise in us
and shout our own orders.

*Cuz, it's them spicy strips and fries*
DJ floats in like his jump shot.

*Bruh, some gizzards and baked beans*
Teré forces in like he's breaking a tackle.

Man, get me
a 16 pc original w/rolls,
lots of rolls.

Maybe 8, or 10,
because it ain't really
about the chicken—
despite the crisp brown skin
that crunches between teeth,
despite the grease
slick enough to shine shoes,
which dribbles its way
down cheeks—

Nah, it's always been the rolls,

so richly fermented
we walk around drunk
off their dough.
No butter,
no honey,
no sauce necessary.
Yeast was enough—
yeast still rising,
yeast always rising,
we try rising,
but are never left
with anything to call ours:

*White boys go there to get their taste*
*of the ghetto,*
Coach Scott says.

Our bodies
sink back
into their seats.

These boys we call peers,
never peeps,
carry a fascination
with consumption:
ivory teeth
crunching brown skin,
they sink in-
to flesh,
working finely tuned incisors,
cannibalistic ire.

They don't understand
that it ain't never
been about the chicken.

# Failed Bomba

¡Ecuajey!

We them
cane canecutters,
them peloteros,
them goya-bean-eating,
always-cooking-
with-too-many-spices-
*I-don't-wanna-smell-that-shit*
muhfuckas.

Them
salsa-and-reggaetón-playing-
siempre-hay-una-fiesta-
*turn-that-shit-down-already*
muhfuckas.

¿Y qué decimos?
*Pa'l carajo.*

We just
malcriaos.
We don't know
no better.
Can't speak English
right,
can't
govern ourselves.

Pero we love our bomba
and
you keep saying *we*
pero tú no eres real—
take out barriles, drum loudest,
drown out anyone who calls out

your mimicry, self-inflicted bullet wounds
to match Filiberto or maybe Daddy Yankee.
How long you practice
those notes, anglo,
that acento?

Think we won't throw you in the ocean?
Let the tiburones pull you apart?
Just keep playing and you'll see.
¿Ecuajey?

# Afro-Seattleite Fragment #1: Black Kid, White City

*Compared with other large U.S. cities, Seattle is pretty white.*
—The Seattle Times

*Reppin' South End seems a death wish.*
—Khingz, "Prodigal"

1.

you are black
wabash ave is black
rainier ave is black
henderson st is black
the 7 and the 106 are black
the south end is black
the cd is black
        your city is
black
                              as shutdown school hallways
(school closure is black)
black
                        as gunpowder
(shootings are black)
black
                as plague
(death is black)
        your city is
black

        you are
black

2.

you are not white
the north end is white

broadway is white
downtown is white
west seattle is white
the 49 and 60 are white
        your city is
white
                              as fluorescent lights in school hallways
(good schools are white)
white
                          as cop-gun muzzle flash
(shootings are white)
white
                  as full-feathered angel wings
(death is white)
       you are not
white

       you are
black

       but your city is
white

# Orpheus as El incomprendido

*—after Ismael Rivera*

Voice scratching itself out my throat, tearing the air. Yo
sé esa agonía. Yo sé perder. And this is pain—that I believe
the voice to boil the air into molasses, melaza que
ahoga, drowns the vocal chords. Cursed with such sweet. I'm going
to sing all sugar. Cavity the ears of any who won't leave me solito,
pobrecito, pobre diablo—¿quién reza por mi? This pain? ¿De estar
enamorado? Smitten by the honey dripping down my own chin when
I sing, runoff of each thick note. Only thing I have to sustain me.
Reminding me I've always known how this ends. How I die.
With a song caught in the middle of my throat, all the sound I have
reversing through the air, a symphony of molasses bent
backwards into the voicebox. This clogged larynx forever concert. Choral
reckoning forever on repeat. Fate of any sonero incomprendido.
To drown forever in the sugar of their own voice. Azúcar que no ni
satisface ni alimenta. All in search of the perfect song, canción que tú
no puedes imaginar. Canción that finally reaches the sun without the agony
of this voice dissolving back into the ocean of my body, broken so no one
can resolidify it. Melody lost forever in my spit. Tell me,
is there any torture worse than to lose a song like this body has?
No desamor, no traición, no lágrima or falsely uttered *querido*
could ever equate to the voice abandoning invention. This tall
noise having no end, floating past sky. I'll tell you what it's like
to bubble the air molasses. Nadie me quiere, la dulzura que soy.

# Encyclopedia Entry: Afro-Seattleite,

*or Seattlensis Africanus.* ~~conservation status: endangered~~ native to: cd. other habitats include: south end, rare spottings in west seattle. intrepid in nature; has been known to roam further north into cap hill. shows no fear in spite of history. will walk down henderson under vigil of streetlight despite gossip of jumpings and worse. will herd by the jack in the box on rainier after confirmed shootings. will venture into north end knowing it's not their city. unclear whether species has brain capacity for long-term memory. findings show they have evolved to obtain a camouflage near invisibility. this genetic mutation only seems to work in the south end and the cd, against those who live elsewhere around the city. data inconclusive as to whether this is darwinian flaw on part of *Seattlensis Africanus* or suggests some sort of biological memory to the species' ancestral habitats. ~~habitats destroyed by gentrification~~ habitats under development. migration forced to the south end ~~'til the south end is taken too~~, then further south. conservation status: least concerned.

# Four-Dollar Mofongo, or On Having to Explain Why Puerto Rico Uses American Dollars

1.

Portrait of:
Mofongo.
Golden plátano bowl
drenched in broth
like a heart in blood.

Portrait of:
Girl ready to pay
for the dish,
clutching paper green
as the plátanos
that made it.

2.

In Spanish class,
Patrick is confused,
wants to know why
dead American presidents
haunt Puerto Rican currency.

The instructor,
Catalonian by birth,
her accent more
paella than mofongo,
either does not know,
or does not care—
once told me to use
"real" Spanish, that
*español real*,
when I wrote *boricua*
to denote my origins.

3.

*El Estado Libre Asociado*
translates into “World’s Oldest Colony.”
Don’t trust your Spanish-
English dictionaries
or Google translate
when you get
“The Free Associated State.”
Puerto Rico is U.S. territory.
As in, this land is your land,
this land is...
your land.

When Scott says “Commonwealth,”
I am wrong
not to correct him
with “Colony”.

4.

I can navigate
being the only Black kid
in class.

It is reluctance to speak
during lessons on slavery.
It is teachers asking me
if I am uncomfortable
with Twain’s use of *nigger*
in *Huck Finn.*
It is jokes about the neighborhood
I grew up in
being gang territory.

But being Puerto Rican
is this squeeze
of my heart,
this eruption
of brothy blood
when being told
I am Third World,
when being taught
I am not good enough
for First World American
dollars,
when learning mofongo,
for all its glitter,
is not gold.

For the first time
I am Puerto Rican.

## Rice and Beans

No filet mignon
or lobster bisque

for this Boricua.
When I die

I want my last meal
to be rice and beans.

All I require
is simplicity:

Red beans over
white rice.

The same thing
my father used to eat,

Grandma Thelma—
God rest her soul—

heating up the stove
on 112th and Lexington.

"But, Mom, we had rice and beans
yesterday," my father complained.

"No, Chico, yesterday we had rice and beans;
today we're having beans and rice."

We make do with what we have;
what we lack is pushed

out of our minds.
We adapt,

code-switching masters
dealing with dualities:

like my father
when he duped Grandma Thelma

by switching from
the simple flavors found

in the Spanish
his mother was raised on

to the English tongue
she always had trouble swallowing,

his ingenuity rewarded
with a frying pan to the head;

like me, in Greece,
hoping to avoid the woman

trying to swindle American tourists:
Isorryperoyonopeakymuchoenglish;

like Grandma Thelma,
who left the tropical shores

of her native Puerto Rico
for the cold winters of New York.

Rice and beans
is more than a dish;

it is the complexity found

in the simplicity of a smile

when, at your high school graduation,
your father, tears in his eyes,

tells you that your *abuela*
is shedding her own tears

of joy
in heaven.

I want that spread over my face
when I die.

# Ode To Bob Marley, Ending in Inheritance

*—after Hanif Abdurraqib*

because that summer / I finally learned / what it was / to carry / music / in my dna / to have it sing / in a way that / makes your blood / dance / through your veins / to the point it's fire / I never listened to Bob Marley / much / Bob Marley is / Jamaica / and to me / Jamaica / was always / the fire in my father's / blood / the juvie sentence / he got / for breaking the bones / of the boy / who exposed his father's / affair / or / the morning after / my father / lunged / at him / for disrespecting / my grandmother / how / my grandfather said / my father / could never / live with him / laughed / *you know / you'd probably kill / me / one day* / it's 2011 / and Bob Marley's / "I Shot the Sheriff" / blasts from / some hotdog vendor's / boom box / in SoDo / and with every note / I could see / Kingston & / London & / New York / dancing / through fire / and as he / hands me / a hotdog / my father / says / the chorus / to this famous / song / almost rang / *me shot / the sheriff / but me / didn't / shoot no / deputy* / until someone / told Bob / to straighten that / crooked / tongue / of his / not understanding / the irony / of telling / someone / to sing / a protest song / in / a tyrant's tongue / the same / irony / as my father / carrying / the name of / a father / who left New York / for Miami / and never / came back / dying / in the same city / as Marley / but Bob / that day / I learned / not to blame / you / I learned / what it's like / to have / fire / dancing in your veins / until you have to / spit / it out in song / and when I took / that hotdog / from my father / I knew / he was saying / *son / don't forget / the other island / that birthed / you* / I knew / he was trying / to give / me / an inheritance / that would never / burn

# Afro-Seattleite Fragment #21: Jamal Crawford, or Ode To the Crossover

I don't know any South End kid who ain't
attempt to mimic you least once or twice.
We bent on knees and prayed for arc as smooth,
a dripping jumper, splashing rain through nets—

but more than that, your handles. Ankle break
-er, every twist and turn—this dance that leaves
your partner grasping air. This dribble trick,
contorted limbs—just stunting on the court.

I never could perfect that hectic dance.
Instead, once found myself devouring dirt
another boy kicked off the court. Too late,
my fingertips just grazing hem of shorts,

and I ain't hating. See the beauty here:
my body crashing while another soars.

## Afro-Seattleite Fragment #8: Ken Griffey, Jr., or The Sweetest Swing

Forget the outfield acrobatics:
limbs swimming through stagnant
Kingdome air brought to life
only when the ball
disappeared from view
and reappeared in your glove.
One motion was your definition.

It was never really level,
more a tilt, like the cap on your head
pegged as disrespect to the sport.
Back elbow bent perfectly—you danced.

Not with your legs, of course
(front knee locked,
back foot floating),
but your hips played lead
to your shoulders.
Better than tango,
better than the waltz,
better than the foxtrot—
hips gyrating so fluidly
MJ would've been jealous.

Fluidity focused into your shoulders
and your hips, black hole at your center,
pure energy when bat met the ball—
movement categorized only as sweet.

Ball obeying your black hole,
dark skin. That swing was confirmation
to a kid in the South End
that baseball was his, too,
because baseball was you.

So dance, Jr.
Hips and shoulders.
One last twirl. Home plate,
one last exhibition so sweet:

*Goodbye, baseball.*

# El Conde Sings "Babaila"

Every breath I swallow is another specter,
corpse compressed into my lungs
until I spit it back out in song—
*guarachar means trumpet bodies out of caskets.*

Corpse compressed into my lungs,
reminder someone will spit me out one day.
*Guarachar means trumpet bodies out of caskets*
and what's a casket but the back of a mouth?

Reminder someone will spit me out one day?
Have you ever heard a prieto sing,
wonder *what's a casket but the back of a mouth,*
*place where every suena rests?*

Have you ever heard a prieto sing?
Every breath I swallow is another specter.
Place where every suena rests
until I spit it back out in song.

## Afro-Seattleite Fragment #15: Jimi Hendrix Plays "The Star-Spangled Banner" – Woodstock, 1969

*...this was only the very beginning of a long, violent summer.*
—Aaron Dixon, *My People Are Rising: Memoir of a Black Panther Party Captain*

Distort the note.
Bend it as many ways
over itself
before it breaks.
Don't break it.
Just burn it.
Let it dangle,
let it bleed—
fragile thing
that can't breathe
on its own,
parasite leeching
off symbiosis
between man and guitar.
Douse the anthem
in gasoline,
and let it ash
in smoke.

Your arson
will be dubbed intro
to a soundtrack
named Vietnam.
Jimi, did your muse reside
on foreign soil?
Or did you think of one year ago,
Garfield Park and Madrona Hill
and Black bodies
bending, dangling, bleeding?
Your Central District under smoke,
engulfed in the flames

that have always seared it,
that have always seared us?

When any ask why you dipped
their precious anthem in gasoline
and allowed smoke rise,
do you tell them this tune
always sounded like a purge to us?

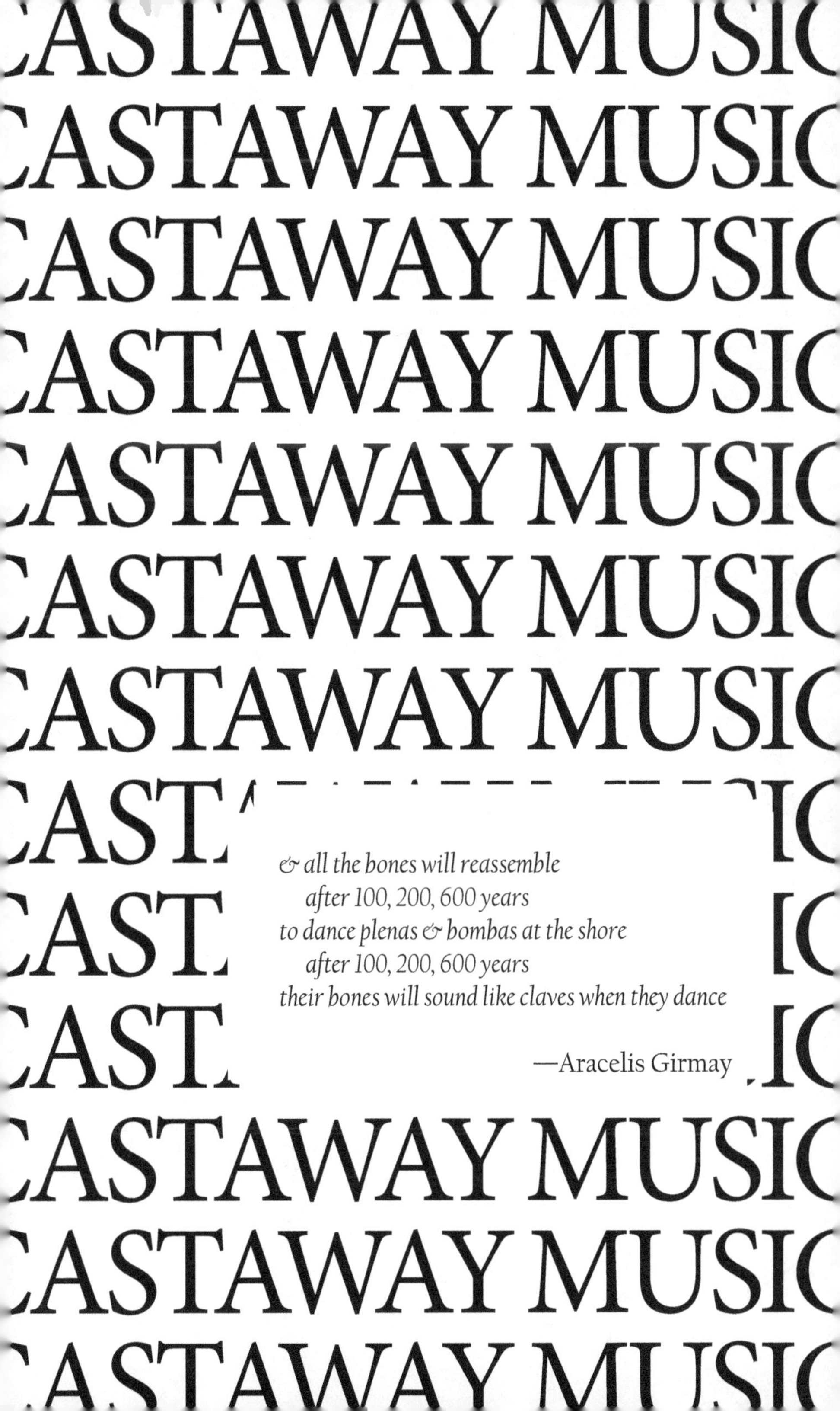

CASTAWAY MUSIC
& all the bones will reassemble
after 100, 200, 600 years
to dance plenas & bombas at the shore
after 100, 200, 600 years
their bones will sound like claves when they dance
—Aracelis Girmay

# Bomba-Blues Dream Sequence

The Bomba Man and The Blues Man want me to play a set.
The Bomba Man unstraps and sets down his tattered leather drum
and The Blues Man stretches his beaten-down guitar
against it and they tell me *Escoge, Choose*. And I still hear the echo
from their last duet, how the strings bounce off the drum's skin,
  make ghost
out of the atmosphere, bend the soundwaves, wonder how I'll help
  this jam

session expand. And I'm aware of how this has always been my
  jam—
choosing between percussion and string, pound and stroke. So I sit,
fully aware that the audience is waiting. Do they know what goes
on in my blood? How often I'm told to choose between a barril's
heartbeat and the breath of guitar strings? How often echoes
of both slosh around in my veins? My English name picks guitar

and bluesy murmurs pound my ears so of course I turn guitarra
into cuá, try to beat this drum with it but the sound jams
itself down my ears and into the crowd. And the boos echo
against my skin, this piel café. How the notes sift
into my tissues and as they crawl through my genes I drown
in the crowd's harsh glares. How I take this as sign they want
  drum's ghosting.

And I pick up the cuá, think the *trucutú trucutú* fantasma
will make up for my failed bomba but hear *Pa'l carajo* and grab the
  guitar,
try to pluck its strings with the stick and my eardrums
tell me what I already know: how the crowd will jeer and jam
their disapproval in my face. My stomach starts to unsettle
and I can feel The Bomba Man and The Blues Man's fingers echoing

inside of me, pounding my colon, strumming my intestines 'til they
  echo

like the perfect duet, blending of leather skin and string, singing
niche spirituals
all throughout my insides. My lungs fill with their song, make my
breath set
fire and I'm forced to repent for my failed blues, fall to my knees,
drop the guitar.
The Blues Man cradles it, instructs *Boy, don't you know the feeling is in
the funk, enjambed*
*notes and chords?* The Bomba Man tells me *It's in the harmony of subidor
and buleador,*

*m'ijo* as he reclaims his cuá and saunters off, dragging away his
misused drum.
And as the two start to play again I hear their lesson, how the
guitar-strings echo
tie themselves around the heavy wood of the drum. How their
perfect descarga
has never been about separation, but about letting all the ghosts
rise from their sleep and sing. And as The Blues Man's fingers glide
the guitar
I realize the audience are those ghosts, cheering on how The
Bomba Man's hands set.

And how could this set be anything but dream? Hypnotism of drum
aided by ethereal float of guitar notes. And of course I hear its echo
as I wake. I'm always chasing ghosts—can't you see that's my jam?

# Bomba-Blues Noise Report

*Crime: Bad bomba and blues playing*

*Witnesses: The Bomba Man and The Blues Man*

*Suspect:*
*Malcolm*

My music is too loud.
I'm disturbing the neighbors.
Each night an officer at my door—
he has learned my name, won't say it,
hopes each night the last,
prays he'll forget this dark boy,

my body like this sound—a disturbance.

The Bomba Man avoids me in the hall
and I hear: *Este tipo, sabes, keeps us up all night.*
The Blues Man shuts his door at me:
*Lawd, ain't nothing you can do about the mess?*
Can't hear me beg bendición, this descarga
no jam session, but hands folded pleading prayer,
anointing of drum and guitar, makeshift limbs—
they can't keep ignoring me, can't keep calling

my sound—this body—disturbance.

I just want one night with no officer,
one night when The Bomba Man
and The Blues Man listen to my song in full.
I can't sleep without their approval,
so I play: *won't you say I belong?*
But I'll never hear them sing along—

# The Bomba Man Talks Shit To Malcolm

You rice and beans
without the onion.
You chuleta
with no adobo.
You bomba
with no cuá.
Puñeta, you just an anglo
with brown skin
and kinky roots—
don't think your roots
mean you owed shit.

With your *I don't dance salsa,*
your *We don't have money for Puerto Rico,*
your *My mom doesn't speak Spanish,*
your *Yo sólo hablo bits and pieces* ass.

Fly Puerto Rican flags,
call the island Borinquen,
cook as much bacalao as you want
but in the end
you as Puerto Rican
as *West Side Story*,
as Puerto Rican as Vanna White.
No bomba, no plena.
You the fading paint
on old shacks in La Perla,
the planes jetting from San Juan
every hour.

You treat your Boricua
like excessive rum:
down it for the buzz,
puke it out the next morning,
go about your day.

Mamabicho, you don't know
this dispossessed homeland,
don't know orgullo means
shouting *wepa* through the vergüenza
of your vomit-stained breath.

# America

*for Rita Moreno*

*Immigrant goes to America,*
*Many hellos in America;*
*Nobody knows in America*
*Puerto Rico's in America!*

1.

Dad doesn't talk about his pain,
won't tell me the bad stories.
Most of the time,
I have to hear it from Mom:
how her family never liked him.
Her grandma said he only proposed
to get a green card, didn't know
he was American as her.
My older sister's named after her.

Dad told Mom about an ex
with a racist father who said
he had the worst black blood
and white blood,
being Jamaican and Puerto Rican.

Dad never told me what to do
when white boys and black boys screech
*¡ay ay ay qué qué muchacho!* at me,
exaggerate an accent
while making jokes about the machete
I've gotta have, the violence
that's gotta define me.
Maybe that's why I freeze.

2.

I read once Rita Moreno thought her Oscar
from *West Side Story*
would open up more roles for her.
No more playing Conchitas.
She didn't work for seven years.
*After West Side Story,*
*it was pretty much the same thing.*
*A lot of gang stories.*

Dad always hated
*West Side Story.*

*Rita's the only Puerto Rican in it,*
he says. *She don't even play María.*

3.

The one time Dad told me,
shared his pain with me,
it was about the day he got home
from Vietnam. The best friend he'd lost.
The white man shouting slur at him.
Hadn't even changed from his uniform,
beat the man unconscious
in front of a police officer
who had enough pity to tell Dad to leave
before he had to arrest him.

He doesn't tell me
what the man called him,
like I can't imagine it.
Can't hear *spic* over and over—
*Stupid spic! Soldier spic!*

Dad snapping at *spic*,
beating the man over and over,
pounding his head into concrete
over and over.

Like I can't see Rita Moreno
staring in the mirror every morning
of the seven years she didn't work,
lines from *West Side Story*
playing over and over in her head—

*Nobody knows in America*
*Puerto Rico's in America!*

Like I can't see Dad
trying not to remember
what it's like to beat a man bloody
with just his hands.

# The Blues Man Talks Shit To Malcolm

Don't talk about blackness
like you Black.
Save me your broad nose,
nectar-laden lips, and nappy roots—
What you know about this?

Miss me with that
*My mom descends from slaves* bullshit.
I look like I give two fucks
about your mama?
Huh, lightbright,
redbone, decaf negro,
house slave?
Ain't no dip in your step.
You blues with no grain,
blackspeak with no swag.

You think this your birthright
'cause a Black woman bore you?
Mimic our mannerisms
and vernacular
all you like;
you just minstrel show
with a Spanish twang.
Stick to your dale's,
your wepa's,
your compaí's.

Ask yourself:
you really want to claim
this body?
Extension of the poplar tree,
we grow leaves
from fingertip branches.
Flowers bloom in our throats—

where you think blues come from,
anyway?
The soul?
Nah. It's always been
this ravaged, leaf-pricked body.

## Ode To Stevie Wonder, or Mom Calls Me after Milwaukee and All I Can Do Is Listen To "I Wish"

And, no, this isn't the first time she's called

worried I might not be alive.

Isn't the first time she's felt her bones compress

and think the blood around them

is sitting heavy as one of her children

sits heavy in the street.

And she remembers Milwaukee.

How Dad came home bloody one night

after he and a couple other friends got chased

out a bar a white friend brought them to.

Shouts of *Who the hell let these niggers in here?*

stinging his cuts and purpling his bruises.

And haven't our cuts stayed stinging,

our bruises kept singing purple?

And it doesn't matter that Marques

is the one in Milwaukee and not me

'cause aren't me and Marques the same to her?

Black sons who don't call home enough

in a time when Black children are left

bleeding out in the street.

And I almost cry when she says

*You know I had to check in on everyone.*

And when she hangs up I play Stevie Wonder,

"I Wish," over and over again.

Let my headphones hum in my ears.

And I can feel the soundwaves in my body

like a hug. And I think about my own nappy-head

boyhood. How Mom used to cut my hair.

How I used to complain about the sting

on my scalp. And I think this

is what all Black mothers wish.

For their children to be children and safe.

Sting of a haircut the worst offense against our bodies.

And I think maybe before Trayvon. Tamir. Aiyana.

And I think maybe we were never children. Never innocent.

Learned too early to accept these stinging cuts,

these purpling bruises. And I wish we didn't learn so young

the taste of our own blood, the splitting of our own skin.

# Ode To the Barbershop

call it oxymoron     where *to shed*     means     *to gain*
dead weight     of curls
falling to floor in waves—
this be baptism     by blade     or maybe phoenix reburst
birth by burn     of razor     and astringent     where *astringent* means
*yeah, your ass needed a cut*     and     *fuck happened to your line nigga?*
*thrown*     *from seller*     *to customer*     and
first time I sat in the chair     was summer     freshman year of college
I didn't know     the name of the haircut     I wanted
stuttered something vague     about taking it low     and nodded
at everything Tony said     in response     hoped he wouldn't
fuck me up     would keep me fresh     and fitted     place where *fitted*
just means     *fitting in*     means     *what won't I do*     *for the benefit*
*of a lineup?*     means     *I knew I belonged*     *when I said nigga*
*and didn't choke*     *on this mutt blood*     where *this mutt blood*
means     *one time*     *a barber laughed*
*nigga your light-skinned ass must be swimming in bitches*     where *nigga*
means     *I swallowed my tongue*     *in response*
*and the bubbling in my throat*     *matched the hum*     *of the razor*

# Poem in Which Marcus Stroman Addresses Puerto Rico on the Issue of His Puertorriqueñidad, Revolving around a Line from Tato Laviera

Call me a traitor, but I prefer island—
like you, distant pebble in the sea.
Memory is the ocean I have to cross.
The pain of this necessary voyage:
too many graves call for my bones.
I understand that hope is fragile,
but I'd rather not assign politics to a fastball.
The bat splinters the same no matter my jersey;
the ball's stitches still callus my fingers.
That is the only purity I know. How
these battered hands remind me rebelling
*against the mob of stars took me nowhere.*
These battered hands. Remind me rebelling
is the only purity. I know how
the ball's stitches still callus my fingers,
the bat splinters the same no matter my jersey,
but I'd rather not assign politics to a fastball.
I understand that hope is fragile,
but too many graves call for my bones—
the pain of this necessary voyage:
memory. The ocean. I have to cross
you, distant pebble in the sea.
Call me a traitor, but I prefer island.

# The Bomba Man and The Blues Man Argue Over Who Has to Bury Malcolm's Body

his lengua is yours
guitarra strings tied together
only fitting you lower his cajón
dress his cuerpo cacofónico proper
como un padre a su niño

his arms are yours
flailing against skin of drum—
when those arms lose their rhythm
make sure the earth will take him
sing songs with him forever

reverb of bone and tissues

let those huesos vibrate
settle bien fácil into dirt
play a few notes for him
catchy, fast, melodía del espíritu
and maybe his body will follow

until the tissues disappear
echo out into wind
one last song to bring him peace
help the breeze carry his phantom
maybe he'll finally learn a dance

one thing he can call his own

pound a tambor for him
soft leather echoing soft flesh
this isn't entierro, but belén
creak of coffin last-plucked strings
his brazos were mine

play a few notes on them strings
let the sound fade like a heartbeat
homegoing, final family reunion
dirt dropping last percussion
his tongue was mine

all that's left of the body is his

## Grifería: Clemente Responds To Luis Palés Matos

*Yo soy niche, / orgulloso de mis raíces / de tener mucha bemba y grandes narices*
—Tego Calderón, "Loíza"

*Los negros bailan, bailan, bailan*
*ante la fogata encendida.*

Black people dance
to burning effigies in the darkness,
orange flames flicker-flirting
with the sky's black skin,
with our black skin.
We must all dance,
ancestral rhythms pulsing
through fango-mud-bound bodies.
Ñam-ñam todos somos.
But what of me?

*Los negros bailan, bailan, bailan*
*ante la fogata encendida.*

Jazz, blues, calypso,
rumba, bomba and plena—
we dance, dance, dance,
bodies swaying back and forth
with Caribbean waves,
cinnamon-melaza mirrors
to river of black,
the pez de plata moon
silver fish bearing witness
to this pasa, this tuntún,
its eye burning bright
as the fire it observes:
tum-cutum, tum-cutum, indeed—
ba-doom, ba-doom—

but what of my dance?
¿Si ñam-ñam yo no soy?

*Los negros bailan, bailan, bailan*
*ante la fogata encendida.*

I do not dance
with effigies.
Son of the cane cutter,
I have seen the machete
smiling with sunlight
as it swings and slices;
pelotero-ballplayer, my bat swings
no rhythmic ancestral motion,
but still in step with Caribbean waves,
in step with the pez de plata moon,
silver fish swimming
through the sky's black skin,
through my black skin,
my bomba-calypso-blues.

Is my tuntún
too off beat?
Was my body not sculpted from mud,
fashioned with the same sediment
seeping from earth?
Am I not allowed to dance?

## Afro-Seattleite Fragment #19: Ode To Gabriel Teodros, or Mixed Kid Learns to Sing

*—after Rita Dove*

We both know *it never stops: the alarm*
*going off* that lets everyone know we don't fit.
You say you were too light to be Black.
For me, it was Brandon, in the middle of our pew.

Telling everyone in Church I couldn't be Black
'cause I'm mixed. Back when he was still my friend.
Didn't matter my dad is half-Jamaican
like his mom. Too much salsa singing

on his skin, *a thicket in its own making*
that kept the words caught in my throat
when I had to hold Brandon's hand
during prayer and that's when I learned

*each phrase returns.* In college Tariq
says I wouldn't understand Chief Keef
'cause I'm not really Black and he ain't even
that much darker than me. I had to finish

the last lap in Mario Kart with nothing
but the stupid Rainbow Road flutes whistling at us
and I'm thinking this is why we turn to song.
*No chord is safe* 'cause we ain't never been.

Dissect instruments and turntable alive and *the notes*
*stack themselves onto* our skin. Bleed black
onto us. Name us something new 'cause old blood
never took us, our half-breed cries—

*There were no wretched sounds. The music*
*pulls higher and higher*

## Fried

*—after Kevin Young and Kimberly Grabowski Strayer*

1.

Seattle, summer,
75 and sunny,

Mom has sent you
out to play

with Mook and Ronk.
The golden rule:

Give her the day
as she gave you life;

don't come back
until dinner

and when you do
get back,

keep your skinny butt
out of her kitchen.

Sweat has already
taken hold of her hair.

Roots nappy as yours,
best not try traverse them.

*I don't care*
*if you're thirsty.*

*I don't need more bodies*
*in this hot kitchen.*

But you can't help it.
Your ears sizzle

to the tune
of that crackling oil,

sweeter than any siren's song,
more earthy, more blues,

like normalcy with big
punctuation marks

of struggle and there it is,
golden brown,

perfectly crispy
like the smack

upside your head
Mom gives you,

the jolt crackling
like oil in the pan.

2.

Mornings away
are cold,

the nights
colder,

though warmed
by mofongo:

slices
of plátano

fried golden,
then mashed with

chicharrón and garlic
under a pestle's weight.

The action
is listless—

no, it's persistent,
insistent on binding

as much as breaking.
Like the boleros,

tales of heartbreak
Dad boomed

from any CD player
harder than his machismo,

his bravado, his
*¡ahí-ahí!*

This was meant
to bind him to Mom,

demonstration that he is not
just sharp salsa,

that even the greenest plátano
can be broken down.

You exist only
in front of them.

That is,
these sliced-up plátanos

(nose sparking
to the garlic of this grind,

the crackle of wood-
smashed chicharrón),

but maybe also
those boleros,

Ismael and Celia and Cheo
grinding your soul

under the weight
of their voices,

Cheo, especially,
voice a croon stretching notes

over drums and maracas
that crackle like oil.

3.

Maybe you belong to both.
Maybe mofongo

is fried chicken,
the rhythm

of light and dark
and oil,

the rhythm
of crackle—

Cheo's voice
is Mom's hand

upside your head
is chicharrón.

Plátanos exist
to be fried.

Chicken exists
to be fried.

You exist
in front of them.

You that oil.
You make it all crackle.

## Prayer as Don Omar

Padre nuestro,
que estás en el cielo,
santificado sea tu nombre,

venga un dembow—
fantasma, echo of Santurce tin houses
banged into existence,

castaway music.
Every night shouts and bullets
bouncing off of bodies.

Bodies bouncing off of houses,
off each other, off the waves
and this is what a guaya

sounds like. Beach as soundboard.
Breakage of sand
to 3 + 3 + 2 snare.

Grain and drip bien pegao.
When a barrio drops the bassline
and lights itself like a vela,

a rezo. Un rosario por los prietos.
Took their chains and built
those Santurce tin houses.

Took the leftover scrap metal
and tricked it out into looped blin blin.
Listen to the slide of their feet

as they dance on the ocean's breeze.
Put all their weight onto the humidity
until the dembow finally drops.

# Ode To La Sista, or I Listen To *Majestad negroide* and Reread Palés Matos

*¡Sús, mis cocolos con negras caras!—*

This is the bámbula we've been waiting for.

I'm pulled into the bombazo as "Rulé candela" plays,

try to time my feet's tapping to this tuntún, this rumbling

that can only come from a dozen pairs of feet pounding dirt together—

rhythm of bones, this percussive skeleton a perpetual sound funnel.

And as the air between my joints vacuums in the bass

I'm reading "Majestad negra" and think this was Palés Matos's vision,

the Puerto Rico he imagined. Soundboard his Quimbamba verdadera—

this layered percussion what the Antilles burns for, like each kick snare

is a sugarcane field set ablaze.

La Sista, I wonder—are you too good for Palés Matos?

Caught up in myth and mulatas, rivers of sugar and molasses,

could he have ever seen you coming? Imagined something as sweet

as this dembow? Us prietos finding our
Quimbamba in a drumkit,

squeezing every bámbula and ancestors' bones

into this dembow's dust.

# Ode To Tego Calderón, or The Day *El abayarde* Dropped Was Maelo's Resurrection

it isn't the salsa-backed intro
on the cover, mirror held up
nariz into boca, drip molasses
to el sonero mayor. sonero-
no bomba interludes
maelo owned in villa palmeras
the *ecuajey* you sing like him
*tú eres guasa guasa* we
los prietos los niches
played back in reverse
taking place on stage
*negra son un desfile*
*se alegra*

horns heralding his salsa vieja
*esto fue lo que trajo el barco*
to bemba. voz is drenched in it
improv mutates over breakbeat
bring us back to santurce
the "witinila" sample
your nod to loíza and
direct to puerto rico
styled yourself abayarde
hand pushing out of casket
singing one more time
*de melaza en flor que cuando*
*de su negrura todo*

the fro you sport
the way you dip
make you vocal copy
and dembow ricochet
rumbones de esquina
in "salte del medio"
los difuntos and the cry
a los afroboricuas los negros
and maelo's entierro
nazareno clutching mic
*las caras lindas de mi gente*
*pasa frente a mí*
*el corazón*

# Afro-Seattleite Fragment #18: When I Found Out *Cold Hearted in Cloud City* Is a Love Letter To the South End

Maybe it started like anything—
joke, homeboys chilling,
listening to "Black Han Solo."
Why not smoke out that swag,

these clouds, this city?
It's about time The Town learned
what it meant for us have that Souf
stuck rooted in our guts.

It goes back to boyhood,
before I started thinking coffin or escape.
When I stole peanut butter cups
from the corner store with Yonas.

One of us always played distraction.
Asking how much Choco Tacos cost
while the other stuffed pockets and our
fingers tracked the evidence.

Goes back to fake fights with Brandon
that turned into real fights. The time he took
the Gameboy from my sister and I tackled him.
Decided he wasn't no one to fuck with no more

as we wiped our bloodied noses and elbows
and maybe it was just our bruised egos
but we claimed it was
proof we real and here and alive.

I'm in college, bumping "Carbonite Flow,"
in my dorm room on full blast.
Don't care if my roommate walks in.
First white boy I ever lived with—

once asked me if I had to do my hair so loud
as I picked out my fro and
now I see the impulse to shout
*Souf End* over phaser backbeat.

Remember cutting that Souf out my mouth
to survive in high school, deciding
I would never get mad or say nigga
around all those white folks and now

I almost miss the reek of weed on the 7.
Proof I was real and here and alive.
That's why I needed this. Khingz
deeming love poem not enough,

responding with love poem.
My first summer back from school
I stood by Lake Washington.
Threw rocks in the blue and waited

for the echo to throw them back at me.
Shouted *Souf End* and waited
for the echo to shout it back at me.
Thought maybe echo was more than echo,

waited for the South End to say *I love you* back at me.

# Notes

The epigraphs opening the book and its sections, in order of appearance, come from the following sources: "New World A-Comin'" by Kamau Brathwaite, from *Rights of Passage*; "The Weary Blues" by Langston Hughes, from *The Weary Blues*; "bomba, para siempre" by Tato Laviera, from *Enclave*; and "Tucutu Tán" by Aracelis Girmay, from *Teeth*

"Afro-Seattleite Fragment #19: Ode To Gabriel Teodros, or Mixed Kid Learns to Sing" contains both references to "Beautiful" by Gabriel Teodros and lines from Rita Dove's "Robert Schumann, Or: Musical Genius Begins with Affliction," from *The Yellow House on the Corner*

"America" contains lyrics from the West Side Story Song of the same name

"The Bomba Man and The Blues Man walk into a bar," contains lyrics from Roberto Angleró's "Si Dios fuera negro" and Robert Johnson's "Cross Roads Blues"

"Clemente al Sonero Mayor: Elegy in Bomba" contains lyrics from "El negro bembón" by Cortijo y Su Combo, of which Ismael Rivera was the lead singer

"Grifería: Clemente Responds To Luis Palés Matos" contains lines from Luis Palés Matos's "Candombe," from *Tuntún de pasa y grifería*

"Lamento en bolero (Clemente's Pain)" contains lyrics from Cheo Feliciano's "Cansancio"

The opening line from "Ode To La Sista, or I Listen To Majestad negroide and Reread Palés Matos" is from "Majestad negra" by Luis Palés Matos, from *Tuntún de pasa y grifería*

"Ode To Tego Calderón, or The Day El abayarde Dropped Was

Maelo's Resurrection" contains, along with references to multiple songs from El abayarde, lyrics from "Las caras lindas" by Ismael Rivera y Sus Cachimbos"

"Ode To Zion & Lennox in Which I Consider My Dad otra vez, Ending on a Lyric by Cheo Feliciano" contains lyrics from Cheo Feliciano's "Mi triste problema"

"Orpheus as El incomprendido" is a golden shovel based on the opening of "Incomprendido" by Ismael Rivera y Sus Cachimbos

"Poem in Which Marcus Stroman Addresses Puerto Rico on the Issue of His Puertorriqueñidad, Revolving around a Line from Tato Laviera" contains a line from Tato Laviera's "against muñoz pamphleteering," from *La Carreta Made a U-turn*

"Promesa" contains lyrics from "Promise" by Romeo Santos, featuring Usher, and is a reference to the Puerto Rico Oversight, Management, and Economic Stability Act (PROMESA)

# Acknowledgments

Many thanks go to the editors and journals that first featured these poems and previous versions of them:

*The Acentos Review, Aethlon: Journal of Sports Literature, Beech Street Review, Bird's Thumb, The Boiler Journal, Breakwater Review, City Arts, The Collagist, Connotation Press, Crab Creek Review, Crab Fat Magazine, CURA: A Literary Journal of Art and Action, Drunk in a Midnight Choir, fields, Fjords Review: Black American Edition, IDK, Juked, Kweli Journal, Label Me Latina/o, Maps for Teeth, Moko, Pacifica Literary Review (Online), Nashville Review, Queen Mob's Teahouse, Sediments Literary-Arts Journal, The Shallow Ends, SiDEKiCK LIT, StepAway, Vanderbilt Review, Vinyl Poetry & Prose, Winter Tangerine Review, Words Apart,* and *Word Riot*

"Afro-Seattleite Fragment #6: Prayer in the Mode of Sir Mix-a-Lot's 'Posse on Broadway,' or South End Kid Returns To Capitol Hill Six Years after Graduating High School" was selected by the Visual Poetry Project for their 2017 video series, and translated into a short film by Matthew Ericson

"Afro-Seattleite Fragment #21: Jamal Crawford, or Ode To the Crossover" was selected by Seattle Civic Poet Claudia Casto-Luna to be included in a map featuring poems inspired by the city of Seattle

"Ode To the Barbershop" was published by Backbone Press as winner of the 2016 Lucille Clifton Poetry Prize.

A number of these poems also appear in the chapbook *mxd kd mixtape*, published by Glass Poetry Press.

Thank you to my family, for all your love and support. To my parents, Michael Friend & Jerrilyn Fowler, for all your encouragement, and to my siblings, Nini, Veronica, and Marques.

Thank you to Inlandia Institute. To Cati Porter and Cynthia Arrieu-King for making this book a possibility.

Thank you to all of the teachers who have helped shape my work. To Beth Bachmann, Angie Cruz, Lynn Emanuel, Sandra María Esteves, Rick Hilles, Dawn Lundy Martin, Terrance Hayes, Willie Perdomo, Shalini Puri, and Autumn Womack. With special thanks to Yona Harvey, whose advice and guidance helped me through numerous versions of this book, and Imani Owens, who helped me envision different ways of looking at music, diaspora, and blackness.

Thank you also to all of my classmates at the University of Pittsburgh, for all of your kindness and care in helping me work through many of the poems in this book. Immense gratitude goes to Cameron Barnett, who very frequently has been the first eyes for a number of poems; to my cohort, Matthew Carlin, Stephanie Cawley, Sam Corfman, and Kimberly Grabowski Strayer, who struggled and thrived together with me as family, and pushed my craft immensely during my time in the program; and to Kazumi Chin and Michelle Lin, who have been a constant source of support and inspiration. Thank you for being my peers and my friends.

Thank you to the homies and family who continually keep me grounded. To my fellow Black Plantain, JR Mahung. To Alfredo Aguilar, Jubi Arriola-Headley, Ariana Brown, Denice Frohman, Eduardo Gabrieloff, Sarah Rafael García, April Gibson, Yalie Kamara, Raina J. León, Sheila Maldonado, Nate Marshall, Mark Maza, Jasminne Méndez, Lupe Méndez, Jessica Lanay Moore, Yesenia Montilla, Nuri Nusrat, Christina Olivares, Ola Osinaike, Ana Portnoy Brimmer, Noel Quiñones, Gabriel Ramirez, Julian Randall, Peggy Robles-Alvarado, Brittany Rogers, Steffan Triplett, Laura Villareal, Anna Weber, and Javier Zamora. Thank you for continuing to push me to be a better poet and person.

Thank you to all of the spaces and organizations that have supported me and helped me to produce this work. To CantoMundo, VONA/Voices of Our Nations, the Center for African American Poetry & Poetics, the University of Memphis/Talbot International Writing Awards, and my very first writing family, Vandy Spoken Word.

Thank you to Emily Albi, Jordan Alcantara, Lyka Allen, Shelby Bautista, Katarina de la Cruz, Yessica Hernandez-Cruz, Chris Hufana, and Olga Morales-García, my very first readers.

And, of course, thank you to Gabrielle Ralambo-Rajerison, who continues to ground and challenge me with both her art and her love.

# About the Author

**Malcolm Friend** is a poet originally from the Rainier Beach neighborhood of Seattle, Washington. He received his BA from Vanderbilt University, and his MFA from the University of Pittsburgh. He is the author of the chapbook *mxd kd mixtape* (Glass Poetry, 2017) and the full length collection *Our Bruises Kept Singing Purple* (Inlandia Books, 2018), winner of the 2017 Hillary Gravendyk Prize. He has received awards and fellowships from organizations including CantoMundo, VONA/Voices of Our Nations, the Center for African American Poetry & Poetics, Backbone Press, and the University of Memphis.

## About the Inlandia Institute

The Inlandia Institute is a regional non-profit literary center. We seek to bring focus to the richness of the literary enterprise that has existed in this region for ages. The mission of the Inlandia Institute is to recognize, support, and expand literary activity in all of its forms in Inland Southern California by publishing books and sponsoring programs that deepen people's awareness, understanding, and appreciation of this unique, complex and creatively vibrant region.

The Institute publishes high-quality regional writing in print and electronic form, including books published in partnership with Heyday under the Inlandia Institute imprint, as well as independent Inlandia Institute publications. The Inlandia Institute is also home to the Hillary Gravendyk prize, a national and regional poetry book competition.

Inlandia presents free public literary programming featuring authors who live in, work in, and/or write about Inland Southern California.

We also provide Creative Literacy Programs for children and youth, and hold creative writing workshops for teens and adults.

In addition, every two years, the Inlandia Institute appoints a distinguished jury panel from outside of the region to name an Inlandia Literary Laureate who serves as an ambassador for the Inlandia Institute, promoting literature, creative literacy, and community throughout the entire Inlandia region. To date, Laureates include Susan Straight (2010-12), Gayle Brandeis (2012-14), Juan Delgado (2014-16), and Nikia Chaney (2016-2018).

To learn more about the Inlandia Institute, please visit our website at www.InlandiaInstitute.org.

# Other Inlandia Publications

**Inlandia Books - Literary**
*Go to the Living*
Micah Chatterton

*Traces of a Fifth Column*
Marco Maisto
Winner of the 2016 National Hillary Gravendyk Prize

*God's Will for Monsters*
Rachelle Cruz
Winner of the 2016 Regional Hillary Gravendyk Prize

*Map of an Onion*
Kenji C. Liu
Winner of the 2015 National Hillary Gravendyk Prize

*All Things Lose Thousands of Times*
Angela Peñaredondo
Winner of the 2015 Regional Hillary Gravendyk Prize

**Inlandia Books - Community**
*Henry L. A. Jekel: Architect of Eastern Skyscrapers and the California Style, 1895-1950*
H. Vincent Moses
Catherine Whitmore

*While We're Here We Should Sing*
The Why Nots

*No Easy Way: Integrating Riverside Schools - A Victory for Community*
Arthur L. Littleworth
Edited by Dawn Hassett
Foreword by Dr. V. P. Franklin
Introduction by Susan Straight

*Tia's Tamale Trouble*
Julianna Cruz, author
Tracie Lents, illustrator

*Orangelandia: The Literature of Inland Citrus*
Edited by Gayle Brandeis

*Dos Chiles/Two Chilies*
Julianna Cruz

Yearly, *Writing from Inlandia:*
*Work of the Inlandia Creative Writing Writing Workshops*
Edited by the Inlandia Institute Publications Committee

**Heyday Inlandia Imprint Books**
*Empire*
Lewis deSoto

*Vital Signs*
Juan Delgado and Thomas McGovern

*Rose Hill: An Intermarriage before Its Time*
Carlos Cortès

*No Place for a Puritan: The Literature of California's Deserts*
Edited by Ruth Nolan

*Backyard Birds of the Inland Empire*
Sheila N. Kee

*Dream Street*
Douglas F. McCulloh

*Inlandia: A Literary Journey Through California's Inland Empire*
Edited by Gayle Wattawa with an introduction by Susan Straight

Inlandia Electronic Publications
*Inlandia: A Literary Journey, an on-line journal*

INLANDIA
BOOKS
LITERARY

CPSIA information can be obtained
at www.ICGtesting.com
Printed in the USA
LVHW091752311019
635967LV00005B/782/P